Tea Ceremony

asian arts & crafts for creative kids

Shozo Sato

Assisted by Alice Ogura Sato

Tuttle Publishing

Tokyo • Rutland, Vermont • Singapore

CAUTION: The projects in this book require boiling water and brewing hot tea, which can cause serious physical injury if handled improperly. Children should be supervised carefully and provided with any assistance they need to insure their safety around hot water.

First published in 2005 by Tuttle Publishing, an imprint of Periplus Editions (HK) Ltd., with editorial offices at 364 Innovation Drive, North Clarendon, VT 05759 and 130 Joo Seng Road, #06-01, Singapore 368357.

Library of Congress Cataloging-in-Publication Data
Sato, Shozo.
    Tea ceremony / Shozo Sato; assisted by Alice Ogura Sato;
[illustrations by Masturah Jeffrey]. -- 1st edition.
        p. cm. (Asian arts and crafts for creative kids)
    ISBN-13: 978-0-8048-3500-8 (hc.)
    ISBN-10:0-8048-3500-4 (hc.)
    1. Japanese tea ceremony. I. Sato, Alice Ogura. II. Jeffrey, Masturah, ill. III. Title.
GT2910.S3673 2004
394.1'5--dc22   2004010253

Distributed by

North America, Latin America & Europe
Tuttle Publishing
364 Innovation Drive
North Clarendon, VT 05759-9436
Tel: (802) 773-8930
Fax: (802) 773-6993
info@tuttlepublishing.com
www.tuttlepublishing.com

Japan
Tuttle Publishing
Yaekari Building, 3rd Floor
5-4-12 Ōsaki
Shinagawa-ku
Tokyo 141 0032
Tel: (03) 5437-0171
Fax: (03) 5437-0755
tuttle-sales@gol.com

Asia Pacific
Berkeley Books Pte. Ltd.
130 Joo Seng Road
#06-01 Olivine Building
Singapore 368357
Tel: (65) 6280-1330
Fax: (65) 6280-6290
inquiries@periplus.com.sg
www.periplus.com

First edition

09 08 07 06   10 9 8 7 6 5 4 3 2

Printed in Malaysia
Illustrations by Masturah Jeffrey
Text design by Kathryn Sky-Peck

contents

Acknowledgments

Over the four-hundred-year history of the tea ceremony, hundreds of valuable books have been published. I consider myself merely an interpreter of this great practice of *cha no yu* and introducer to the Western world, especially to young people. In creating this book, I owe much to the following people: my teacher Kishimoto Kosen, who has been my mentor for over a half century; from Dai Nippon Chado Gakkai Headquarters in Tokyo, both Ehara Shou, for her scholarly guidance, and its president, Tanaka Seno, author of *Tea Ceremony,* a well-known book originally published by Kodahsha; Tanaka Misho of Chado Gakkai School, who is teaching the tea ceremony at the Kikuzawa Higashi Elementary School of Shika numa City, Tochigi prefecture; Anzai Chizuko of the Urasenke School, who teaches at Sanbonmatsu Elementary School of Hachioji in Tokyo; Professor Kimiko Gunji of the Japan House, University of Illinois, for photography; and the children. Photographs were taken by Shozo Sato at Zakyu, a center for Japanese arts in northern California.

The simple enjoyment that can come from drinking a beverage is a pleasure that we often experience without much thought. We might remember a nice drink associated with a special situation, however. A warm cup of hot chocolate may be especially wonderful after coming inside from playing in the snow, and a cold glass of lemonade may be nice on a hot summer day. These occasions are even more enjoyable and memorable when the setting is comfortable and we are able to share the moment with someone special.

In Japan, a special tradition was developed to create a calm and wonderful atmosphere for drinking tea. This tradition is called the tea ceremony. It is based not just on sharing a cup of tea with a friend, but on experiencing a special moment in a very relaxing kind of place.

This may sound like a strange idea, but it might be similar to something you already do. For example, imagine the following situation:

Your friend comes over on a warm summer day and you decide to have some orange juice. You ask your friend to sit at the dining room table. Perhaps you set out a nice vase containing a flower, or at least remove the newspapers and clutter from the table. You go to the refrigerator and take out the pitcher of juice with the simplest movements of your hands and body, without spilling a drop. With care and grace that you aren't even aware of, you place the juice container on the countertop.

You know that the juice is orange, so perhaps you pick glasses that will complement the color of the juice. You pour juice into the glasses, being careful not to splash juice on the counter. You might even wipe the pitcher with a napkin after you've finished pouring. Without thought, as if it's the most obvious thing in the world, you return the container to the refrigerator.

When you place the glass of orange juice in front of your friend, it's like you're telling him or her to "please enjoy" the juice. Your friend will probably thank you for the juice, but even if nothing is said, you know that your friend appreciates your thoughtfulness. And if you've taken the time to enhance your experience – by adding ice to the glasses, or clearing the clutter off the table – you and your friend will share a pleasant, refreshing moment.

This sort of act is performed often. We're so used to this conduct that we do it almost without thinking.

The tea ceremony focuses on how people can find pleasure, peace, and companionship in a simple and beautiful way – but in a more organized way than when you and your friend enjoy glasses of juice on a warm day. This spirit of the tea ceremony is the essence of Japanese culture.

This book first presents a short history on the tea ceremony and then takes you through all of the steps for making a bowl of tea to share with friends.

preface

Japanese children enjoy a tea ceremony.

Schoolchildren enjoy tea at the Japan House at the University of Illinois.

Children both in Japan and in the United States have experienced and enjoyed the tea ceremony, and perhaps you can, too.

I will present the tea ceremony as it is traditionally performed, using the traditional tools. You may need to modify some of the steps with what is available to you. The traditional ceremony calls for *matcha,* which is a powdered green tea. You must also have a whisk for the powdered tea.

Serving brewed tea is another kind of ceremony. Brewed tea is often served in very casually, but there are also more formal ways to serve it. Steps will be included so that you can serve brewed tea in more formal ways.

I take great pleasure in presenting the tea ceremony to you. I sincerely hope that you will share what you learn in this book with your friends, as sharing is the spirit of the tea ceremony.

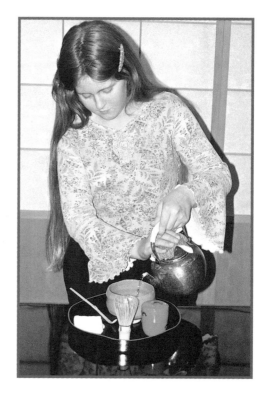

Trieste practices the tea ceremony in northern California.

Tea, or *cha*, is a beverage that people in Asian countries have been drinking since ancient times. The earliest tea trees were found growing along the borders of southern China and in a country known today as Myanmar. During the sixteenth century, Dutch and Portuguese traders introduced tea to the European countries. Today people all over the world drink tea.

For many generations in Japan, tea has been enjoyed in a specially arranged artistic setting and served in an artful manner. The tea ceremony is a way for people to come together, not necessarily to talk or play, but to find calmness and peace of mind. The host and guest come together to appreciate the offering and the receiving of the bowl of tea in a small room. Only a few pieces of equipment are used, and everything is arranged in a way that creates harmony and beauty. Because the tea room has only a few things on display, one can enjoy the beauty of each object. One can also fully appreciate the taste, fragrance, and sounds of the tea. In a tea ceremony, tea is served in a way that will bring pleasure to all five senses of both the person serving tea and the person drinking it.

Left to right: wa, kei, sei, jaku

What Is a Tea Ceremony?

The spirit of the tea ceremony is based upon four special ideas: *wa*, which means "harmony"; *kei*, which means "respect"; *sei*, which means "cleanliness" or "purity"; and *jaku*, which means "tranquility." When you include all four elements, you can fully enjoy the beauty of simply drinking a bowl of tea.

In creating a setting of this harmony, it is important to think about what wa, kei, sei, and jaku mean. To start, what kind of setting gives you a sense of harmony and peace? This would probably be a place that is without clutter and is very clean. In a tearoom, there is often just a simple flower arrangement. The flowers are used only to enhance or honor the vase or container, which is often a work of art in itself.

Next, respect comes when everyone and everything is treated with thoughtful consideration. For example, if you are having a guest who has very special needs such as a physical disability, you will make special arrangements. In the tea ceremony, this is called *kokoro ire* (*kokoro* means "heart" and *ire* means "putting in"), which means that you are putting your heart into the activity. You are being thoughtful and considerate of your guests. You will then have a setting that is very peaceful. These are things you can do in any social situation.

In a tea ceremony, you do not discuss things that can lead to arguments, such as which sports team is best. Only such things as the tea equipment or the meaning of the calligraphy are discussed. This helps to maintain a peaceful atmosphere. The pouring of cold water into hot water, the placing of a bamboo dipper on a stand, the gentle sound of a bamboo whisk whipping tea, and even the gentle sipping of hot tea are all sounds to be appreciated.

How the Tea Ceremony Developed

The history of the tea ceremony began when Eisai, a Buddhist monk, brought tea plants from China to Japan in A.D. 1187.

Eisai, who studied Zen Buddhism in China, learned that the monks practiced a ritual of drinking tea as a way to stay alert while meditating and stay healthy. When Eisai returned to Japan, he brought back tea seeds and seedlings from China and shared the tradition of drinking tea with the Japanese monks.

From the tea plants Eisai planted grew a whole culture of tea in Japan. As time passed, tea was enjoyed not just by the humble monks but also by the very wealthy. During the fourteenth and fifteenth centuries, a special tea drinking game was developed by the wealthy warrior classes. This game was called *To-o Cha*, which means "tea competition."

In To-o Cha, one tastes a variety of teas and tries to guess the district where each type of tea came from. This game took place in only the wealthiest of houses, most often the homes of military generals, with extravagant decorations and delicious meals. Unlike the modest ceremony of the monks, this tea ceremony was very much about showing off one's wealth. Those who could afford it would decorate their large homes with paintings by famous Chinese painters and other arts and crafts produced in China. As many as a thousand pieces of tea equipment and fine works of art were exhibited at a single To-o Cha gathering.

This extravagant display was eventually replaced by a daisu, a portable shelf used in a *hiroma*, a large room about 15 square feet. Only the necessary pieces of equipment were displayed on the daisu. The guests were seated in the same room as the host, who conducted the tea ceremony while they watched. This was much different from the earlier ceremonies, in which the hosts prepared tea in a separate room. The host's preparation of the tea in front of the guests changed the very meaning of the tea ceremony, bringing forth the spirit of sharing.

By the end of the fifteenth century, tea was becoming more available, and the general public could create their own versions of the tea ceremony.

Many people helped transform the tea ceremony into what it is today, but the following people were among the most influential.

Murata Shuko: A Buddhist monk, Shuko was the first person to hold tea ceremonies in a small room with only a few guests. Shuko emphasized the "study of humbleness" and disapproved of showing off wealth.

The merchants of Sakai: This class of wealthy traders also held tea ceremonies in small rooms with few guests. The settings of their tea ceremonies were peaceful and simple. The merchants of Sakai were the first to use Japanese folk crafts in tea ceremonies instead of ones imported from China.

Sen no Rikyu: A Sakai merchant, Rikyu was a student of Taken Jo-o, who was famous for his tea ceremonies. When they prepared their tea ceremonies, both men took into account the season, the time of day, and the social occasion. Rikyu organized the steps for preparing bowls of tea that are still used today. His ceremonies emphasized modesty, spirituality, and the beauty of simplicity.

Tea leaves come in many different forms, depending on where they are grown, the month when the leaves are picked, and the way they are processed. Green tea is the most popular tea in Japan, and is the tea used in the traditional tea ceremony. However, other varieties of tea are also popular. Since there are many kinds of teas, each with a very different flavor, it is important to understand the different types of teas and how each should be prepared to get the best flavor.

Dan cha

Dan cha is considered the oldest type of green tea. In Japanese, *dan* means "brick" and *cha* means "tea."

To make dan cha, the tea leaves are steamed and then placed in a mortar and pounded with a pestle to release the juices that help hold the pieces together. The clump is then molded into a square or round disk and dried. This dried-brick form of tea is much easier to transport than loose green tea leaves. Originally, dan cha was the main way that people drank tea, unless they grew the tea bushes themselves.

When drinking dan cha, the necessary amount is broken or cut off from the brick, crushed into small, grainy pieces, and boiled in water. In some countries, such as Mongolia, Tibet, and remote parts of China, ingredients such as milk, salt, dried citrus skins, rice, or butter were added to bring out the essence of the tea. In Japan, however, nothing is added to the tea. This boiled tea led to a category of tea called *sen*, which means "boil" in Japanese. The following categories of green tea are produced in Japan today.

Dan cha

Matcha

Matcha is a type of very finely powdered green tea. Tea leaves for matcha are grown in a special way: The tea plants are covered with bamboo curtains to shade the tender new leaves from direct sunlight until after the leaves are picked. This treatment allows the young tea leaves to develop the least amount of bitterness. Only two or three of the leaves are handpicked from the plant, steamed lightly, and then dried. Once the leaves are dried, they are kept in darkness for six months to allow the flavor to develop.

Matcha or powdered green tea

Traditionally, when matcha was needed, only the necessary amount of tea leaves were taken out and ground to a fine powder in a small stone mill by a very heavy stone. Today, one can buy powdered green tea in an airtight container. Matcha should be refrigerated after opening the container, since otherwise it will soon lose its flavor and color.

Drinking coarsely ground tea was developed in China from the ninth to eleventh centuries, during the Sung Dynasty. This practice of drinking coarsely ground tea was brought to Japan along with Zen Buddhism. Today, drinking of matcha during a tea ceremony occurs only in Japan or in countries where the Japanese tea ceremony is practiced.

Gyokuro

Tea leaves for *gyokuro* are produced and processed in a way similar to matcha. The tea plants are pro-

tected from direct sunlight by bamboo screens until the leaves are picked.

Gyokuro is the highest quality of leaf green tea, and so it requires the greatest care in preparation. The young tea sprouts that grow in partial shade produce a sweet flavor that high temperatures will destroy. It is important that you use cooled water when making gyokuro. First bring hot water to a boil, and then transfer it to a ceramic vessel and wait until the water cools down. If you misjudge and use very hot water, the leaves will lose their sweet flavor and your gyokuro will be bitter.

Sencha

Tea leaves for *sencha* are left on the stems for a longer period of time than for gyokuro. During the

Fresh leaves and processed leaves. Left to right: gyokuro with very young leaves; sencha with more mature leaves; bancha, hojicha, and genmai cha all come from the large mature leaves

processing, the surfaces of the leaves are broken so that the flavor and nutrients of the tea will be released when the tea is steeped. The leaves become a beautiful shiny dark green and have a wonderful fragrance.

More hot water is used for brewing sencha than for gyokuro, so be sure to use larger cups. The water temperature should be adjusted according to the grade of tea: the lower the grade of sencha, the higher the temperature of the water.

Bancha and Kukicha

Ban means "night" in Japanese, and *bancha* is harvested late in the season. After these high-quality tea leaves have been harvested, the rest of the leaves are left to grow in the sun until late summer. Today, mechanical trimmers and a vacuum bag are used for mass harvesting. The leaves, which are in many stages of growth, are blended with the stems. Sometimes the very small stems are separated to make *kukicha*. Bancha and kukicha are the least expensive types of green tea.

Bancha should steep for about 30 seconds. Boiling the tea leaves in hot water will bring out the full flavor. The teacup for serving bancha should be larger than one for serving sencha.

Hojicha

Inexpensive tea leaves are sorted and divided into various categories. In Japanese, the word *hoji* means "toasted." When leaves are toasted, it is called *hojicha.* Freshly toasted tea produces a wonderful aroma and is commonly served to clear the palate after a meal.

The amount of tea leaves and hot water are the same as for bancha. However, during the brewing process, the tea leaves and hot water can be put in a metal teapot and brought to a boil for one minute. The teacup for hojicha should be a large and heavy ceramic cup so that the cup will not become too hot for your hands to hold.

Genmai cha

Rice, roasted like popcorn, can be mixed with lower-grade sencha to make *genmai cha*. The fragrance and flavor of roasted rice makes genmai cha a popular beverage to serve after a meal.

Kocha or Black Tea

Black tea has been the most popular tea in the West since the seventeenth century. Since then, Japanese culture has been influenced by the West, and as a result, black tea has become extremely popular in Japan, too. Japanese people who enjoy a Western lifestyle will often serve black tea, rather than green tea, or coffee during their social gatherings.

Countless varieties of black tea have been produced by different countries around the world. After the tea leaves for black teas have been harvested, they are placed in the shade for a much longer time than for green teas so that chemical changes take place. The tea leaves are steamed and then dried. This long process eventually turns the tea leaves black and removes the bitter taste.

There are many famous brand names of black tea, such as English breakfast, Queen Mary's, and Earl Grey. In Japan, all of these are called *kocha* and are served in the same way, often with lemon, milk, or honey.

Chinese Teas

In the West, oolong tea is the most well known of the many varieties of Chinese teas. In recent years, oolong tea has become popular in Japan.

After the Chinese tea leaves have been harvested, they are spread evenly on the surface of a large flat container and placed in the shade for a few days. This helps to reduce the bitter taste but still allows some of the nutrients to remain. The wilted tea leaves are then placed on large steel pans over fires that toast the leaves for a short period of time. Then the soft and bendable tea leaves are placed in a cotton bag the size of a pillow case and are kneaded in a circular rotation, much like the way bread dough is kneaded. This process, which takes many hours, breaks down the surfaces of the tea leaves and allows the leaves to roll up. The leaves are then dried.

Chinese tea is unique in that after the leaves have been placed in a teapot, often hot water is poured over them and swirled around a couple of times, but then the hot water is poured out completely. The tea leaves soften and open up, creating a wonderful and fragrant aroma.

Every time you enjoy a cup of tea, you need to use some special equipment. When you're relaxing at home, you usually only need a teapot and a teacup or mug. However, in the Japanese tea ceremony, many special utensils are used to prepare and present the powdered green tea.

The type of equipment used depends on the type of tea ceremony. In a formal tea ceremony held in a hiroma, the equipment is very refined. For example, the use of a perfectly shaped tea bowl on a stand, called a *tenmoku*, expresses the significance of the guest or the occasion. A semiformal tea ceremony uses a symmetrical bowl, like the *Hagi,* or Korean-style, tea bowl. Informal tea ceremonies, which are held in a more rustic and intimate setting, use equipment that may be simple in appearance but still appreciated for their beauty.

Tea Bowls (Chawan)

In the Japanese tea ceremony, bowls are used to drink matcha. Brewed tea is served in cups without handles, and so teacups in Japan are never filled to the top. This way both the upper part of the teacup and the bottom are not too hot, making the cup easier to handle.

Tea Containers or Caddies (Chaire and Natsume)

There are two basic kinds of containers to hold powdered green tea: *chaire* and *natsume*. Chaire are containers that hold thick tea such as *koicha,* the

tea utensils

Left: Informal Oribe tea bowl with an irregular shape. The Oribe style is often characterized by green glaze dripping over a crackled cream glaze. The accidental beauty in design is a special aspect of Oribe. Center: Semiformal Hagi tea bowl in Ido style, originally from Korea. Right: Formal tenmoku tea bowl with a sterling silver rim and a glaze patterned like tiger skin—a style from the Sung Dynasty of China—on a black lacquered stand.

Natsume and chaire (in silk shifuku) in informal, semiformal, and formal styles (left to right)

highest quality green tea, and are usually ceramic with ivory lids. Chaire are placed in a *shifuku*, a bag of fine silk with a cord. Natsume are tea caddies that hold light tea. Natsume are usually made out of wood and then lacquered. Artists take great pride in creating different lacquer patterns, sometimes with gold lacquer and mother-of-pearl designs.

Tea Scoops (Chashaku)

Tea scoops, called *chashaku*, are used to spoon powdered green tea from the tea container into the tea bowl. You should never touch the scoop part of the chashaku with your hand.

Informal tea scoops are made out of bamboo, usually with a bamboo joint in the middle of the handle. Semiformal tea scoops are made out of bamboo or wood, and formal tea scoops are made out of ivory.

Tea Whisks (Chasen)

Made out of a single bamboo stalk, *chasen* are about five inches long with a diameter of one inch or less. The lowest two inches become the handle, and the upper part is split into many fine strands. A whisk for light tea, *usucha*, may have 80 to 200 fine strands. A whisk for thick tea, *koicha*, has fewer, thicker strands.

In November, a special ceremony called *Chasen Kuyo* honors the chasen for carrying out a "function for a noble purpose." People bring their worn-out chasen, which they have used during the year,

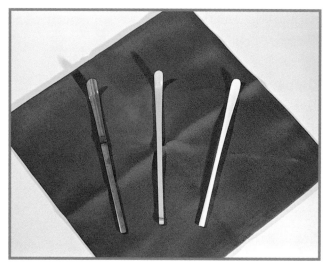

Left to right: Informal, semiformal, and formal tea scoops (chashaku)

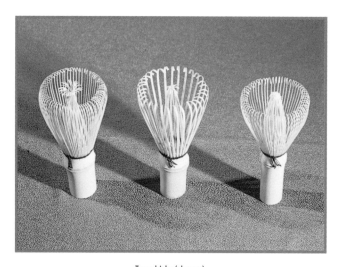

Tea whisks (chasen)

to a Buddhist temple. The priest conducts a Buddhist ceremony to show appreciation for the "labor" that the chasen have performed throughout the year, and then the chasen are burned. Everyone bows in respect.

Dippers (Hishaku)

Hishaku are used to ladle water from the teakettle into the tea bowl. Hishaku are usually made out of bamboo and come in different sizes for different seasons. Winter hishaku are slightly larger and stronger than summer hishaku.

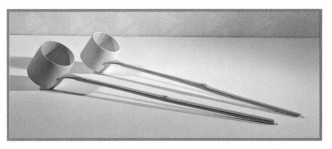

Back: Bamboo dipper (hishaku) used for summer tea. Front: Hishaku used for winter tea.

Small Brocade Mat (Kobukusa)

A *kobukusa* is a very small silk mat of about 5 ¾ square inches that is placed under a tea bowl or other utensils before examining them. Kobukusa come in a variety of colorful and patterned fabrics. Bright colors are used by women and subdued colors are used by men.

If the tea ceremony is held in a large room, an attendant to the host will deliver the bowl of tea to the guest. In such a case, the bowl is placed on the kobukusa, which functions as a tray. In a small tea ceremony room, the guest will usually come forward to receive the bowl.

Also, since the tea bowl can be very hot, the kobukusa can be used to protect hands as the bowl is passed around.

Varieties of beautiful fabrics with origins from ancient China, Persia, or Japan have been faithfully reproduced for kobukusa.

Fukusa

The *fukusa* is a piece of silk cloth about 11 square inches that is used to symbolically clean or purify utensils. Usually fukusa are orange or red for

Fukusa

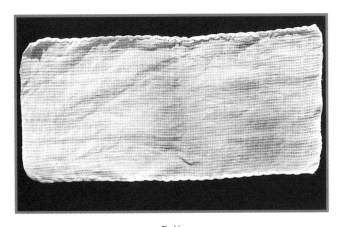

Chakin

Summer-style kama

Winter-style kama

women and purple for men. However, fukusa come in hundreds of colors. Some may have a design, and some may have autographs of great tea masters. Tea practitioners will select a fukusa for a tea ceremony depending upon the occasion, and season of the ceremony, and even the color of the clothing they will wear.

Chakin

The *chakin* is a small, disposable linen cloth, about 5 ¾ by 12 inches, used for wiping the tea bowl. The edges are folded over and hemmed with a stitch.

Teakettles (Kama)

Teakettles, called *kama*, are used to heat the water for tea. In the kitchen we may use a simple teakettle on top of the stove, but in Japanese tearooms, kama are heated over a hearth—a pit about 14 inches square and 10 inches deep to hold charcoal or electric coils—sunken in the floor or on a brazier called a *furo*—a utensil made of bronze or ceramic designed to hold either charcoal or electric coils.

There are two styles of kama: winter and summer. Because a sunken hearth is used in the winter, that kama must be much larger than the portable one used in summer, because it also helps to heat the room. There are many different shapes and textures that a kama can have, but one of the most important qualities is the soothing sound that it creates when the water reaches boiling temperature.

The center teapot is sterling silver, and the right-hand pot is iron. These pots are used for the tray-style and box-style tea ceremonies, and are each about five inches in diameter.

Teapots

Teapots are used in special kinds of tea ceremonies, such as the tray and box styles, or when a kama is not used. Teapots come in many different shapes and styles, so pick one that suits the style of your ceremony.

Flower Vases

A simple display of flowers is important for creating a seasonal atmosphere for your tea ceremony. Flowers and vases are chosen by keeping in mind the season and style of ceremony. Flower vases for the summer season are often bamboo baskets; in the winter, ceramic vases are often used.

Fresh-Water Containers (Mizusashi)

The *mizusashi*, or fresh-water container, is an important utensil in the tearoom. In the summer, a large shallow container of water in the tearoom will create a sense of coolness. These containers can be made of ceramic or wood. In the winter, smaller mizusashi are used and are made of ceramics of all kinds, ranging from porcelain to stoneware.

Waste-Water Containers (Kensui)

Called *kensui* in Japanese, these containers are meant to hold any water you need to discard, including the water you use to warm up the tea bowls.

Flower vases for the summer

Ceramic flower vases

Fresh-water container (mizusashi)

Waste-water containers (kensui)

Futa oki

Lacquered wooden trays

Futa Oki

Futa oki are used in a tea ceremony when a kama (teakettle) and hishaku (dipper) are used. The futa oki is where the lid is placed when the kettle is open (*futa* means "lid" and *oki* means "to rest"). Futa oki come in many different styles and are made from a variety of materials, ranging from sterling silver and cast bronze to ceramics and bamboo. When the hishaku is placed on the futa oki, it creates a tapping sound. This sound announces the beginning of the tea ceremony. Bamboo futa oki must first be soaked in water so that they will make this sound when tapped.

Trays

Wooden trays are sometimes used in tea ceremonies to offer sweet treats to your guests. Also, a book of white paper, called a *kaishi*, is used by the guests. The kaishi serves as a plate for the sweets that each guest receives, and then the top sheet is removed, folded, and then later used to clean the bowl. Another kind of tray is used to hold the equipment used in a tea ceremony.

project 1:
setting up the tearoom

Creating the right atmosphere for your tea ceremony is very important for a successful gathering. Allow yourself plenty of time so that you will not be rushed.

In a traditional tea ceremony, the guests move through five different spaces: the receiving room, the passageway to the tearoom, the space for symbolic cleansing, the waiting area, and then finally the tearoom. Although this sounds like a complicated process, it may not be that different from when you have guests in your home. You first receive your guests at the front door, and then lead them to a room where you will entertain them. You might point out your washroom along the way. If a meal is to be served, you will likely have your guests assembled in another room until the meal is ready.

You would clean and prepare each of these places in a special way, even if only because your parents tell you to. You know that it is polite to have a clean room ready for your guests. This is similar to the preparation that goes into a tea ceremony, but tea ceremonies are very carefully planned for this unique occasion. As you read the instructions for a tea ceremony, remember that these steps can be changed or skipped to suit your own tea ceremony.

Step 1: The Receiving Room (Yoritsuki)

First, a room is prepared to receive the invited guests when they first arrive for the tea ceremony. This room is called a *yoritsuki,* and it is usually part of the host's home. This is where the guests will prepare themselves for the ceremony by using the washroom or, if necessary, changing their clothes. Some guests may wish to wear a kimono, as worn in traditional tea ceremonies.

The host, who doesn't appear until later, usually has set out a pot of hot water, which one of the guests will serve to the others. This water is used to cleanse the guests' palates. Sometimes hot water containing toasted popped rice will be served instead of plain hot water.

The role of the receiving room is to make the guests feel welcome. It is important that the guests are able to relax and get ready for the tea ceremony.

Step 2: The Passageway (Roji)

In the traditional ceremony, after all of the guests have finished their preparations, they will move outdoors to the garden, called a *roji* in Japanese. The roji is a specially prepared passageway that leads to the tearoom. The passageway has flat stepping-stones called *tobi ishi*. The host will have swept the stepping-stones and sprayed the ground with water to create a sense of purification similar to the effect of a gentle rain. This moisture revives the mosses that cover the ground, creating a beautiful green freshness that contrasts with the artfully arranged stepping-stones.

Walking through a tranquil path helps to bring a feeling of peace. Experiencing the beauty of nature is a nice way to prepare for the ceremony.

Passageway (roji)

Step 3: The Space for Symbolic Cleansing (Tskukubai)

Eventually the stepping-stones in the roji will guide the guests to the *tskukubai*, which literally means "squatting down." This area is outdoors and is usually made up of artfully arranged rocks surrounded by pebbles and carefully planted grasses, shrubs, and trees. The arrangement creates a soothing atmosphere.

There will be one large, flat stepping-stone in front of a stone basin into which fresh water is constantly flowing. One at a time, guests will crouch down in front of the basin, pick up the dipper, and dip out water to rinse their hands and mouths. If it is a very cold day, the host will provide a wooden bucket of warm water.

Space for symbolic cleansing (tskukubai)

This physical cleansing helps the guests to feel refreshed in both mind and body. When completed, the guests follow the stepping-stones to the next point.

Step 4: The Waiting Room (Machiai)

After each guest has finished with the cleansing process, he or she goes to a waiting area, called the *machiai*, to wait for the rest of the group. The machiai is a simple structure with a roof and a bench against a wall. While seated, guests quietly enjoy the peacefulness of the garden.

Once everyone has gathered in the machiai, the host, who has been preparing things inside, will appear. All guests stand up and bow simultaneously, without any conversation. The host returns to the tearoom and sounds a gong, the sign to enter the tearoom. The sound of the gong symbolizes the sound of temple

Tearoom and machiai

Entrance to the tearoom (nijiri guchi)

bells coming from deep in the mountains to announce the time of the day. In Japan the huge bronze temple bells with their echoing resonance has been a welcome sound since ancient times.

Step 5: Entering the Tearoom (Chashitsu)

When the sound of the gong fades away, guests rise and the main guest leads the way to the tearoom on the stepping-stone path. Close to the tearoom entrance, the height and size of the stepping-stones begins to change. The stepping-stones here are slightly larger so that guests can stand comfortably to look around and appreciate the overall view of the tearoom from the outside. The stepping-stones lead to a small entrance into the tearoom.

In traditional Japanese architecture, all houses are built about two to three feet above the ground for better circulation of air during the rainy season when humidity is high. To reach the entrance, a higher stepping-stone will bring the guests to face the entrance. The tearoom, or *chashitsu*, has a unique entrance that is only about three feet high and two and a half feet wide. This small entrance is called the *nijiri guchi* (*nijiri* means "to slide" and *guchi* means "entrance"). Whether or not they are important people with titles, all guests stoop to enter this small room, humbled and equal.

The guests who enter the tearoom through this nijiri guchi are already almost in a sitting position, so they will move on to the front of the *tokonoma*, an alcove built in a room and raised about three to four inches above the floor to display the arts. On display might be a beautiful wall hanging of calligraphy, often the work of a known Zen priest. Usually the calligraphy has been selected for display because it carries a message related to this particular tea ceremony. Each guest places a fan in front of his or her knees and bows in respect, and then thinks about the meaning of the calligraphy statement.

A tearoom is generally constructed of wooden beams with a natural finish, and the walls are natural clay. White handmade paper covers the *shoji* windows and sliding doors. This creates a subdued and quiet atmosphere.

Also on display might be a flower arrangement called *chabana,* or "flower for the tearoom," and an incense holder. Chabana is a simple arrangement and flowers should not overwhelm the vase. The incense holders are selected according to the season: In summer, carved wood or beautiful lacquer containers are used; incense containers in winter are usually ceramic.

Guests will examine the artwork, bow to show respect, and then move on to the place where the host will be seated to examine the teakettle (kama) and other utensils on display.

Inside the tearoom, where the host will be seated on the tatami. The setting here is a winter-style tea ceremony. Notice the tokonoma, where the artwork is on display.

The wonderful fragrance of incense flows across the room and the sound of gently boiling water is heard. Soft light comes through the shoji screens and highlights the art objects on display. This space now offers a sense of elegance and peace as guests wait in a quiet state of mind. Guests now take their seating places for the tea ceremony

The host will now open a sliding door which connects the tearoom to the teahouse kitchen, called the *mizuya*, where the preparations for the tea ceremony have taken place. The host enters quietly and places a fan in front of his knees. The guests do the same, and silently they all bow.

The host gives his welcome, and if there is a special reason for the gathering, will give an explanation. On behalf of all of the invited guests, the main guest expresses appreciation for this special occasion.

From this point on, the host, main guest, and the last guest will have the important roles to play. The guests seated between the main and last guests share in all of the activities within the tearoom. A very important statement in the tea ceremony is *ichi za konryu* (*ichi* means "one," *za* means "group," and *konryu* means "become one unit"). This means that during all of the activities that take place in the tea ceremony, guests must be sensitive to the host's movements and steps. The main guest especially must know exactly when and how to coordinate with the host. The host must be equally "in tune" with the guests, and make adjustments accordingly. When the host and guests can reach this understanding in silence, the members within the small tearoom become a unit, and this is called ichi za konryu. In a sense, this spirit is the whole purpose for having a gathering of *cha no yu*.

What to Do at Home

To create a setting for a tea ceremony in your own home, remember that simplicity and cleanliness are important.

1: The Receiving Room (Yoritsuki)

Decide where you would like to receive your guests. This might be the porch, the sitting room, or the kitchen.

Make sure that there are enough chairs for everyone to sit comfortably. Let your guests know where they can put their coats, and let your guests know where the washroom is.

To make the receiving room more inviting, set up a nice flower arrangement or place plants around the room.

Set out some cups and a pot of hot water for your guests. In place of toasted popped rice, you might add a slice of lemon to each cup. If it's a warm day, perhaps cold water would be more appealing. Whatever you decide to serve your guests, it should be light and not too flavorful. You want to get their taste buds ready for the tea.

2: The Passageway (Roji)

Guests will go from the receiving room to the place where you will serve tea. If it is the next room, you will not have a roji. That is okay. Even in Japan, many homes do not have a roji that leads to the tearoom.

If they must go through a hall, then you can make it more like a roji by placing a plant or flowers along the way.

3: The Space for Symbolic Purification (Tsukubai)

You can re-create the experience of the tsukubai in several ways. You might set a bucket or bowl of water and a dipper on your porch or patio where guests can rinse their hands. If guests will go to the next room for tea, you might wet a washcloth (one for each guest), wring it out, and place it on a plate or basket for each guest to use before entering your tearoom. In winter, you might use a hot cloth; in summer, a cool one. Or you could direct guests to your washroom, and leave fresh towels for them to dry their hands.

Wherever you decide to set up the tsukubai, make sure that everything is very clean. Try to bring nature to this area, too, by decorating it with fresh flowers or plants.

4: The Waiting Room (Machiai)

After your guests have washed their hands, they will wait for you to call them to the tearoom. This might be the same room as your receiving room because you may not have another place for them to wait. When you are ready to receive them, invite them into the room where you will serve tea. You can use a bell or chime to represent the gong.

5: Entering the Tearoom (Chashitsu)

Use care when you select the room where you will serve tea. First you must have a special place, most likely a table, where you will place your equipment to serve tea. Your guests must be seated to face you. You will see to it that you have provided enough seating to accommodate your guests, and that everyone will be comfortable. As a good host, you will have removed clutter and cleaned the room very carefully.

When you are preparing your tearoom to receive guests, remember that simplicity is very important. Make sure that the room is clean and orderly. Remove all clutter. In a tea ceremony, flowers are arranged to enhance the vase. Since the vase is to be admired, do not use large bouquets of flowers. If there is already artwork on the walls, it should not be too distracting if you have everything else in order. Clear your table for preparing and serving tea of everything but your necessary equipment.

Once everyone is settled, enter the room and welcome your guests with a bow. At this time all guests should also stand and bow. In Japan, a bow is sign of respect.

If this is a special occasion, let your guests know why you have invited them for tea. An example would be that this is the first day of spring. Once in the room, guests should be quiet and clear their minds of everything but what is in the tearoom. The objects are not to be judged or compared with other objects. Each object should be appreciated for its unique beauty. All controversial subjects are avoided. To enjoy the spirit of the tea ceremony means that you will focus on the moment and on the simple beauty of the utensils or objects on display. In this peaceful atmosphere your guests can enjoy a bowl of tea.

project 2:
starting the tea ceremony

Tea sweets

Once you are seated and ready to begin the ceremony, take several deep breaths. See how calming it is. First, bring in your tray of sweets. In a tea ceremony, the sweets have a lot of sugar but no artificial flavorings. They are bland so they will not overpower the taste of the tea, but are still very beautiful. Guests eat a sweet just before receiving the bowl of tea. This sweetness takes the place of sugar in the tea. Each guest should be given a small paper napkin to use both as a plate and a napkin.

Step 1: When you first bring the tray into the tearoom, it should be covered with a fukusa.

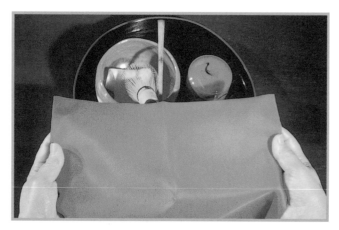

Step 2: Very carefully pick up the fukusa, holding as much of the fukusa as possible in each hand, and lift it off the tray.

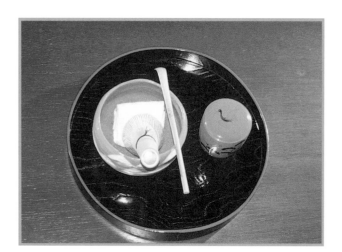

Step 3: When the fukusa is removed, the natsume and bowl with utensils will be in this arrangement.

Step 4: Hold the corner of the fukusa to make this triangular shape.

Step 5: Hold the fukusa in a horizontal position. Your hands should be a few inches from the ends, to give the fukusa stability. With your left palm up, place three fingers on top of the left corner of the fukusa, and your thumb underneath.

Step 6: While holding both corners of the fukusa, move your right hand up over your left hand, so that the right side of the fukusa is vertical.

Step 7: Release your left hand, but try to maintain the fold you created. Slide your left hand up the outside of the fukusa until it reaches your right hand. Form a ring around the fukusa with your left hand, and move it down to the midpoint.

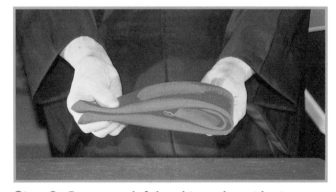

Step 8: Once your left hand is at the midpoint, catch both ends of the fukusa in your right hand. Bring the ends to the right so that the fukusa is in a horizontal position. At the same time, slip the four fingers of your left hand underneath the fukusa. With your right hand, make sure that the ends are even.

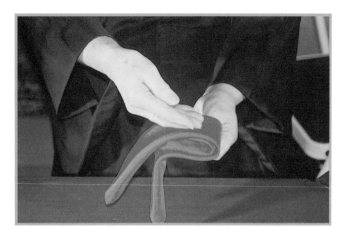

Step 9: Release the ends of the fukusa and gently run the backs of the fingers of your right hand along the contour of your left hand, folding the ends of the fukusa underneath your left hand.

Step 10: Carefully remove the fingers of your left hand from inside the fukusa. Place your left hand in front of your stomach to form a little tray, and place the fukusa in the palm of your left hand. Now you have successfully folded a fukusa in circular form.

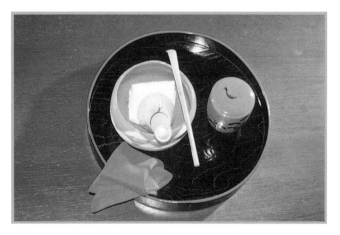

Step 11: Place the fukusa at the seven-o'clock position on the tray.

Step 12: Pick up the tea bowl with your left hand and the natsume with your right hand. Simultaneously, move the natsume up to the twelve-o'clock position and the tea bowl to the six-o'clock position.

Step 13: Now is the time to "clean" the natsume. This is a symbolic cleaning. The fukusa must be refolded following steps 5–10. Then, using both hands, fold the fukusa in half.

Step 14: Hold the folded fukusa in your right hand and pick up the natsume (black in this photograph) with your left hand. Place the fukusa on the lid, at the nine-o'clock position.

Step 15: Move the fukusa from the nine-o'clock position, up to twelve o'clock, and then to the three-o'clock position. Next move the fukusa across the center of the natsume. Then move the fukusa from nine o'clock to six o'clock, and then back to three o'clock.

Step 16: Open the last fold you made in the fukusa and wipe the fukusa across the top of the natsume, moving it from the five-o'clock to the eleven-o'clock position.

33

Step 17: Replace the natsume at the ten-o'clock position on the tray.

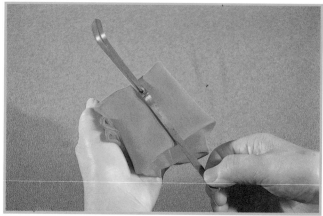

Step 18: Refold the fukusa and place it on your left palm. Pick up the chashaku, or tea scoop, and place it on the center of the fukusa.

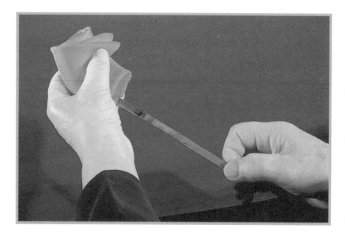

Step 19: Fold the fukusa over the tea scoop and press down, moving the fukusa up to the tip of the chashaku. At the tip, gently press, and then move fukusa away.

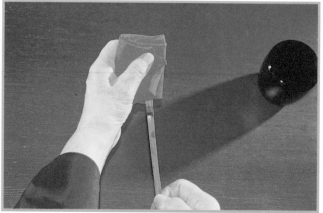

Step 20: Return the fukusa to the base of the chashaku. Move the fukusa past the midpoint of the chashaku and turn your left hand clockwise so that your thumb faces up.

34

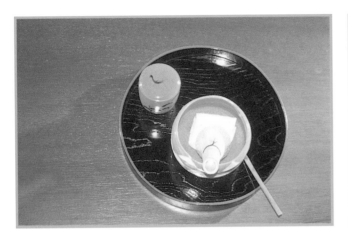

Step 21: Place the chashaku at the five-o'clock position on the tray.

Step 22: Place the chasen, or whisk, at the twelve-o'clock position.

Step 23: Remove the chakin, or linen cloth, from the tea bowl and place it at the one-o'clock position.

Step 24: Return the fukusa to its original place on the tray (the seven-o'clock position), with the ends pointing away from the tray. You are now ready to begin preparing a bowl of tea.

What to Do at Home

The movements during the tea ceremony seem very exact. In fact, they were developed for the "economy of motion," which means that the motions are as easy and efficient as possible. This may be hard to believe! A beginner often appears to be very clumsy because he is trying so hard that he puts in many more motions than necessary. A tea master's movements seem to flow easily because he does not add any unnecessary motions. While you may not be able to perform a traditional tea ceremony right away, remember to stay calm and do your best to keep the steps simple.

1: Plan your ceremony.

You must plan how you will serve your guests. If you are able to find powdered green tea, you will serve the tea in bowls, and you can follow the steps for *Bon Date*, which is the tray style.

If you plan to use loose tea leaves or tea bags, you will use teacups. You may have Japanese or Chinese teacups without handles, but you can also use regular cups and saucers. You will find steps for brewing tea leaves and tea bags on page 50.

If you are serving powdered green tea, you must have a whisk. You may use substitutes, however, for other pieces of equipment. Traditional tea bowls are about 4 ½ inches in diameter and 3 ½ inches in height. You might find some utensils like this in your kitchen. For a tea scoop, you may use a small spoon. One bamboo scoop of powdered tea equals about ½ teaspoon of tea. Powdered green tea must be sifted before it is served because the fine powder packs into lumps and will be very difficult to whip. For a natsume, or container for tea, use a small container about 3 inches high with a lid between 2 and 2 ½ inches in diameter.

If you are serving brewed tea, plan where you will place each piece of equipment. There are specific places on the tray when you serve in Bon Date style. Serving with confidence will put your guests at ease.

2: Prepare your equipment.

Your equipment should be very clean when you bring it out from the kitchen. However, symbolic cleaning is part of the tea ceremony. If you don't have a fukusa, use a smooth cloth napkin or a hemmed piece of cloth the same size as a fukusa. Practice folding your "fukusa" beforehand so you will not feel awkward while symbolically cleaning your utensils.

You may not have a tea tray, but you can use any tray to bring in your equipment. Know where each piece of equipment should go on your tray so that you won't need to stop your movements as you try to think where to place it.

Remember, you will be more graceful if you have practiced beforehand.

project 3:
preparing the tea bowl and whisk

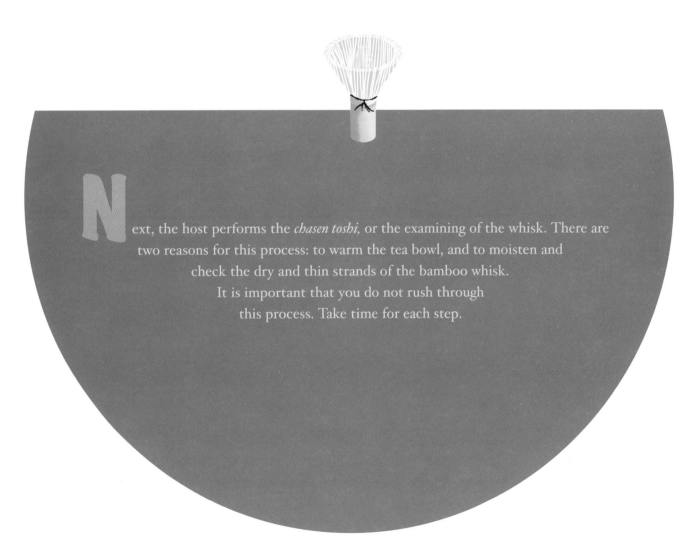

Next, the host performs the *chasen toshi*, or the examining of the whisk. There are two reasons for this process: to warm the tea bowl, and to moisten and check the dry and thin strands of the bamboo whisk. It is important that you do not rush through this process. Take time for each step.

Preparing the Chasen (Whisk)

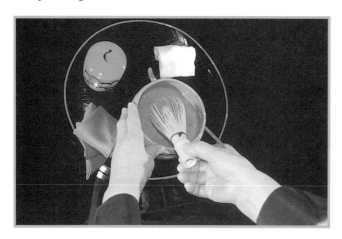

Step 1: The bowl stays on the tray used in the Bon Date ceremony. Pour hot water into the tea bowl. With your right hand, pick up the chasen and place it in the water at the six-o'clock position.

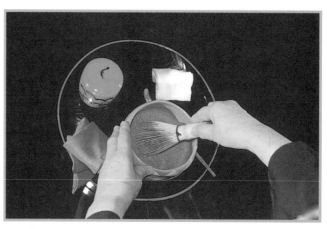

Step 2: With your right hand, move the chasen to the three-o'clock position and gently rest the chasen against the rim.

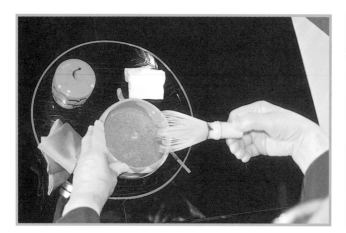

Step 3: Pick up the chasen gently, straight above the tea bowl in a horizontal position, and study the individual strands as you rotate the chasen. Meanwhile, your left hand should hold the tea bowl still.

Step 4: Slowly rotate the chasen toward you until your wrist stops. Then gently lower the chasen back into the bowl and readjust your hand. Repeat the examination three times.

Step 5: After examining the chasen in the air, it is time to moisten the strands. With your right hand holding the chasen, move it from the two-o'clock position to the seven-o'clock position back and forth seven times.

Step 6: Then move the chasen back and forth from five-o'clock to eleven-o'clock a total of five times. Then move the chasen in a circular motion around the inside of the bowl three times.

Step 7: You have now completed the chasen toshi. Notice a black knot on the chasen. Your fingers should be on the knot when the chasen is placed on the tray. When you remove your hand, the black knot faces the guest.

Preparing the Tea Bowl

Step 1: Pour the hot water out of the tea bowl and into the kensui, or waste-water container. Then hold the tea bowl in your left hand, giving your right hand plenty of space for movement. With your right hand, reach for the folded chakin and place it in the center of the bowl.

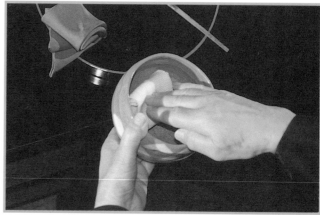

Step 2: Push the corner of the chakin straight back.

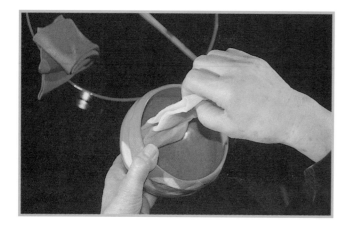

Step 3: With your right hand, grasp the folded edge of the chakin and lift it up. Your thumb should be facing you.

Step 4: After picking up the chakin, turn your wrist clockwise so that your thumb is facing straight up. Drape the chakin over the edge of the tea bowl, at the ten- or eleven-o'clock position of the rim.

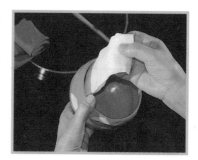

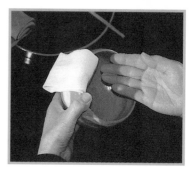

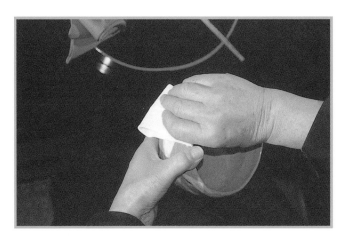

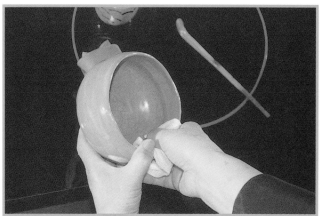

Step 5: Turn your right hand counterclockwise, so that your thumb is in the tea bowl, resting on the chakin, and your fingers are on the outside of the bowl, on the chakin.

Step 6a: When drying the tea bowl, your left hand should remain stationary so that your thumbs touch each other at each turn. While your right hand moves clockwise to dry the bowl, your left hand should hold the bowl firmly.

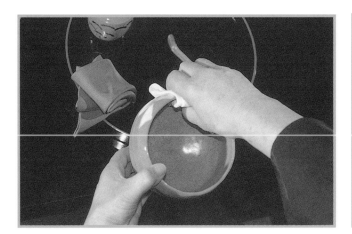

Step 6b: After the first rotation in drying, your right hand should firmly hold the tea bowl to rotate the bowl counterclockwise, while your left hand relaxes its hold. Try not to move the bowl up or down, or to the left or right.

Step 7: Repeat step 6 three times. Turn it a fourth time to readjust the bowl so the front is facing you. Remove the chakin from the tea bowl.

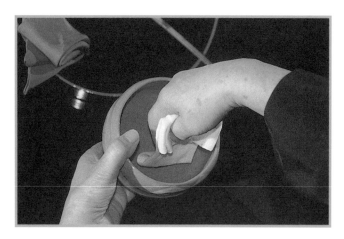

Step 8a: Place the chakin in the bottom of the tea bowl with your right hand.

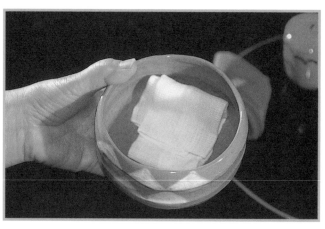

Step 8b: Carefully release the chakin.

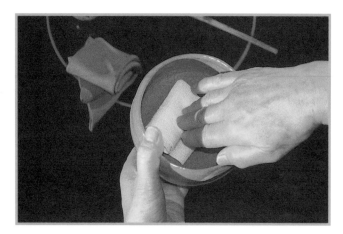

Step 9: Pick up the chakin at the twelve-o'clock position and fold one-third of it toward you.

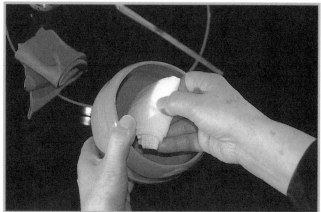

Step 10: Turn your right hand so that your palm faces up and the thumb can be used to pick up the chakin.

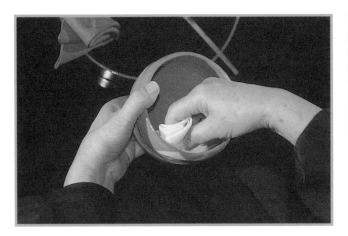

Step 11: Dry the inside of the bowl by first moving the chakin counterclockwise from the twelve- to the six-o'clock positions, and then clockwise from twelve to six o'clock. Then dry the bottom of the bowl with two short strokes: one from the eleven- to the seven-o'clock positions, and one from one to five o'clock.

Step 12: After drying the bowl, place the chakin in the center of the tea bowl. With your right hand, place the tea bowl at the lower-center position (six-o'clock) on the tray.

Step 13: With your right hand, remove the chakin from the tea bowl and place the chakin back in its original position. This completes the drying of the tea bowl.

What to Do at Home

When you plan to have a tea ceremony, it is very important that you decide how it is to be conducted and practice the steps beforehand. Many people spend a lifetime practicing these steps.

However, there are many ways that a beginner can perform a tea ceremony in the spirit of the traditional ritual. Here are a few points to keep in mind:

1: Prepare your equipment.

If you don't have a tea bowl, use a bowl that is about 4 to 5 inches in diameter and 3 ½ inches high. If you cannot find an authentic chakin, use a small white handkerchief. Remember that the reason for this preparation is to warm the bowl and dry it before you put tea in it. The steps may seem complicated, but they were developed to show grace and "economy of motion."

2: Practice, practice, practice.

No matter how informal or untraditional your tea ceremony may be, practice before you perform in front of your guests. You should plan the placement of your equipment on your tray so you can proceed with confidence in front of your guests. This will make your guests feel more comfortable. The discipline that is practiced in a tea ceremony should carry into our daily activities.

3: Plan with your guests in mind.

As you learned earlier, the best hosts carefully consider the special needs and desires of their guests when planning tea ceremonies. If your best friend is allergic to lemons, you can show your thoughtfulness by serving plain hot water before the tea. If one of your friends is in a wheelchair, you'll take special care to make each room of your ceremony easily accessible. If you always remember the importance of kokoro ire, which is putting your heart into the ceremony, you'll always be a wonderful host.

4: Set the mood.

There are plenty of occasions for friends to get together to be loud and energetic, like birthday parties, school dances, or even recess. But a tea ceremony is one of the few special occasions where friends come together to enjoy a moment of quiet and peace. Your friends might enjoy a time when they can appreciate a few simple objects such as a bowl, a vase, and flowers, as well as the taste of tea.

5: Show respect.

Respect is what you show when you are considerate and caring toward your equipment and your friends. This is not something limited to the tearoom, but a behavior we can practice throughout our lives. Over the long history of the tea ceremony, people have taken time out to appreciate the art of things such as a simple tea bowl. If your tea ceremony has some part of this spirit, you have conducted a worthwhile activity.

project 4:
making the tea

Now that all of your tea equipment is clean and your tea bowl is warm, it is time to make the tea for your guests. This requires three steps: scooping the tea into the bowl, whipping the tea, and presenting the tea to your guests.

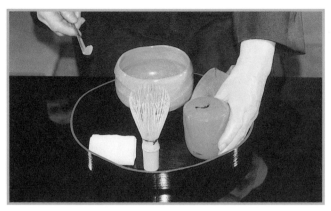

Step 1: With your right hand, pick up the chashaku, or tea scoop. While the left hand approaches the natsume, your right thumb and fingers should move up the chashaku so that your little finger and ring finger can hold the chashaku firmly. Keep the chashaku in a horizontal position, with the top facing up.

Step 2: Bring the natsume above the tea bowl. With the free fingers of your right hand, remove the lid of the natsume.

Step 3: While your right hand lowers the lid onto the tray at the five-o'clock position, your left hand should move the natsume to the nine-o'clock position to the left of the tea bowl.

Step 4: Hold the chashaku like a pencil and scoop out the desired amount. Since powdered green tea is very carefully put into the natsume to form a gently rounded mound, you should not disturb its beauty by dipping into the center. Instead, scoop between the twelve- and one-o'clock positions, along the inner surface.

Step 5: The amount of tea you use will depend upon the guest. For young guests, you might use only one scoop, or ½ teaspoon, because powdered green tea is very concentrated and high in caffeine. For older guests, you may use two heaping scoops. Spread the tea by moving the tip of the chashaku twice across it.

Step 6a: Lightly tap the chashaku against the rim of the bowl to remove excess powdered tea.

Step 6b: After tapping, your fingers should move up the chashuku so that two fingers can hold the chashaku while the other three fingers can pick up the lid of the natsume.

Step 7: After the tea bowl has been warmed and dried, there is still moisture in the bowl. When the powdered green tea is put in the bowl, it may cling to the inside surface of the bowl. Add hot water, using the chasen to release the tea by brushing the bottom of the bowl five or six times.

Step 8: Next, begin rapidly whipping the mixture with your chasen, but do not scrape the bottom of the tea bowl. Whip back and forth twenty-five to thirty times, until you've created a green froth. Break any large bubbles with the tip of your chasen, and then move the chasen to the center of the tea bowl and bring it up.

Step 9: Examine your bowl of whipped tea, and then present it to your guest.

What to Do at Home

The steps above explain how to make a traditional bowl of powdered green tea. However, it may be difficult to find both powdered tea and a whisk. In that case, it will be best to serve your guests either loose green tea or even a tea bag.

Also, when serving brewed tea, sweets are eaten after the first serving of tea.

1: Instead of a teapot with a brazier as your heat source, use a ceramic teapot and teacups. The teapot filled with hot water should be placed on a mat or pad to protect the table surface. You will need a second teapot if you are making brewed tea. Pour hot water in the cups to heat them easily. The grace of a tea ceremony is in eliminating all unnecessary movements as you pour tea.

2: In the pot in which you will brew tea, put in the proper amount of tea. Use one lightly mounded teaspoon for each ¾ cup of hot water. This will serve two to three people, depending on the size of the cups. Steep for a few minutes. Pour a small amount of tea into each of the cups. Continue pouring small amounts for each guest until the pot has been drained.

Even if you do not have the traditional equipment for the tea ceremony, it is still fun for you to follow some of the steps, such as using a chakin or properly folding a fukusa. One day you may even have the opportunity to seriously study the tea ceremony with a teacher.

The beauty of the tea ceremony is in the spirit with which you carry it out. Your sincere concern and wish to enjoy a moment of peace with your guests can be carried out even in the most basic tea ceremony.

project 5: completing the tea ceremony

The closing of a tea ceremony should also be graceful, but now your movements will be faster. Up to this point, guests have been quietly observing and appreciating the simple things around them, and they are physically and spiritually content. This is a time when guests might ask about the history of the tea equipment. You might find it interesting to discuss whether you and your friends find the tea ceremony to be a worthwhile activity.

Step 1: If your guests have had enough tea, bow and say, "I will finish." Remember that young guests should not have more than one bowl of tea, since it is high in caffeine.

Step 2: As the bowl is returned, briefly examine it to see if there is any tea left in it and how much water is needed for rinsing, and then place it on the tray. Pick up the fukusa with your left hand.

Step 3: Hold the hot lid of the teakettle with the fukusa while you pour a small amount of water from the kettle into the bowl.

Step 4: Rinse the bowl by rotating it clockwise. Then pour the water out.

Step 5: Pour more hot water into the bowl. Pick up the chasen and lower it into the bowl at the six-o'clock position. Move the chasen to the three-o'clock position and rest it on the rim of the bowl.

Step 6: Pick up the chasen so that you are holding it horizontally over the bowl.

Step 7: Examine the chasen by making one complete turn with your wrist, and then place the chasen in the bowl. Repeat this step.

Step 8: Briskly clean the chasen in the water, and then remove it from the bowl. Place the chasen in its original position on the tray.

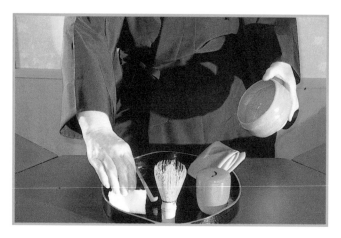

Step 9: With your left hand, pick up the tea bowl and pour the water into the waste-water bowl, or kensui. With your right hand, pick up the chakin.

Step 10: Bring the tea bowl close to your body and place the chakin in the bottom.

Step 11: Place the chasen in the bowl in its original, six-o'clock position. Pick up the scoop with your right hand, and then pick up the fukusa with your left hand.

Step 12: Place the scoop against the top folded corner of the fukusa. While your right hand holds the scoop, let the fukusa drop.

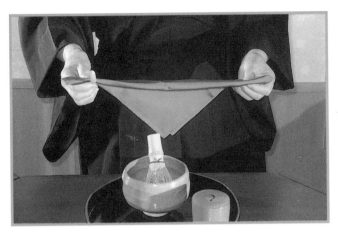

Step 13: Follow steps 5–10 of Project 2: Starting the Tea Ceremony (pages 31–32) for the proper folding of the fukusa. Only this time, hold the scoop against one end of the triangular fold of the fukusa.

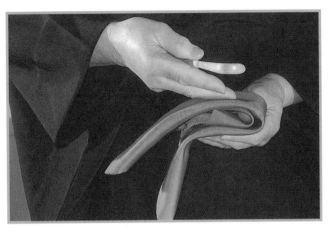

Step 14: Fold the fukusa in half, bringing your left hand to the center of your body.

Step 15: With your right hand, fold the ends of the fukusa under your left hand. Grasp the folded fukusa with your right hand and place it on your left palm. The scoop remains into your right hand.

Step 16: With your right hand, place the scoop on the center of the folded fukusa.

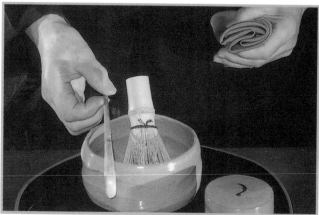

Step 17: Fold the fukusa over the scoop. Press gently, release, then slide the fukusa to the tip of the scoop. Clean the scoop a second time, but this time clean the sides: At the midpoint of the scoop, move the fukusa over to the top of the scoop and continue to the tip.

Step 18: With your right hand, place the cleaned scoop on the rim of the bowl. Continue to hold the fukusa in your left hand.

Step 19: Move the fukusa to the left and dust it lightly over the waste-water bowl to remove loose powder, and then return it to its original position on the tray.

Step 20: Using both hands, simultaneously move the bowl and the natsume back to their original positions with the bowl on the left and the natsume on the right on the tray.

Step 21:
Pick up the folded fukusa with your left hand and pass it to your right hand.

Step 22: With your right hand, use the fukusa to partially open the lid of the kettle.

Step 23: Place the fukusa in the palm of your left hand, but this time with the ends facing up. With your right hand, pick up the top layer of the fukusa, and insert your fingers into the top fold.

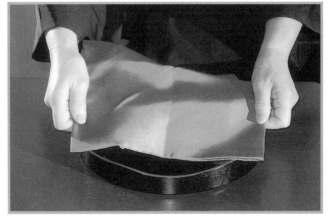

Step 24: With both hands open the fukusa, spreading your fingers to hold it steady. Carefully lay the fukusa over the tray, as it was positioned at the beginning of the tea ceremony.

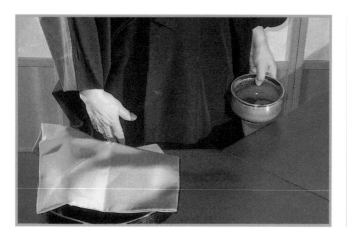 

Step 25: Carry the kensui, or waste-water bowl, out of the tearoom first. Hold it in your left hand.

Step 26: Sit down, and then pick up the tray and carry it out. After the tray has been removed from the tearoom, come back in and bow to your guests. You have completed your tea ceremony!

At the close of the tea ceremony, I hope that you and your guests have enjoyed the gathering.

What to Do at Home

1: At the close of your tea ceremony, tea bowls or cups should be returned to you.

2: The cups, spoons, and other equipment should be placed on the tray in an orderly way, similar to the way they were when you first brought everything in.

3: If you wish, you may rinse the cups with water and empty them into a waste-water container. However, if you have had many guests, by this time you might not have enough water left to rinse your cups. In this case, simply place them on your tray in an orderly way.

4: If you have rinsed your cups, carefully wipe them with a clean, smooth napkin or tea towel. Wipe them with "an economy of motion" and your movements will be more graceful.

5: Take the waste-water container out of the room first. If you have a fukusa, you may cover your tray before carrying it out next. If you do not have a fukusa, it is fine to carry it out uncovered. However, if you wish to cover your tray, use a clean, fresh napkin or towel, not the one you used for drying utensils.

6: Return to the tearoom and bow to your guests. Perhaps this is a time when you can discuss the tea ceremony with your friends. You might discuss whether a ceremony that includes harmony, respect, cleanliness, and tranquility is something you would like to enjoy often in your life.

Final Words

One ancient Chinese saying states, "Youth becomes old easily; accomplishing study is difficult. While you are daydreaming by the riverbank in spring, already the leaves foretell the coming autumn." This statement means that any study is difficult and seems to have no end. The discipline of the tea ceremony also takes a lifetime of study to master. Yet the journey brings rewards, because there is always more to discover and rediscover—not only in the beauty of the craft, but in sharing the simple joy of drinking tea with your friends.

I hope that this introduction has opened your eyes to another way of seeing the world. What you have learned in this book is merely a scratch on the surface, as any form of study must begin with basic information, and often even that is difficult to grasp. The tea ceremony is challenging, but the rewards are great because your lessons and discoveries are shared with your friends. When you practice the tea ceremony in a "spirit of harmony, respect, cleanliness, and tranquility," your friends will appreciate it even more. In my experience, my guests will often say that they have never experienced such a peaceful and enjoyable occasion. The simplicity of the equipment and decoration of the tea ceremony allows minds to think about the natural beauty of things they may not have noticed otherwise. Remember, it is not a grand display of artwork that impresses people here, but the simplicity and beauty of the smallest items. Bringing attention to these things is the most important part of the tea ceremony.

I hope that you have enjoyed this book and have discovered something new. I hope that I have started a ripple in your life with a drop of powdered green tea.

glossary

bancha: green tea harvested late in the season; *ban* means "night"

Bon Date: a style of tea ceremony; *bon* means "tray" and *date* means "to make"

cha: tea

chabana: flower arrangement for the tea ceremony

cha no yu: Japanese tea ceremony

chaire: tea containers for thick powdered tea

chakin: small linen cloth used to dry the tea bowl

chasen: tea whisk

Chasen Kuyo: special tea ceremony for disposing of old whisks

chasen toshi: examination of the whisk

chashitsu: the tearoom

chashaku: tea scoop

chawan: tea bowl

daisu: portable shelf used to carry selected tea utensils

dan cha: oldest kind of tea; brick tea

fukusa: square silk cloth used to clean tea utensils symbolically

furo or brazier: an artfully designed, portable container to hold a heating element

futa oki: rest for the kama lid when the kama must be open; *futa* means "lid" and *oka* means "to rest"

genmai cha: a mixture of sencha and roasted rice

gyokuro: highest-quality green tea

hagi: a kind of ceramic produced in southern Japan

hiroma: large room, about 15 square feet, often used for the formal tea ceremony

hishaku: dipper

hojicha: tea made out of toasted leaves; *hoji* means "toasted"

ichi za konryu: unity created between the host and guests through the tea ceremony

jaku: tranquility

kaishi: soft sheets of paper in a stack used for holding sweets and wiping the tea bowl

kama: teakettle

kei: respect

kensui: waste-water container

kobukusa: tea mat; a square piece of silk, usually brocade

kocha: black tea

koicha: thick green tea

kokoro ire: putting your heart into an activity

kukicha: inexpensive green tea made from bancha stems

machiai: waiting area before the tea ceremony takes place

matcha: powdered green tea

mizusashi: container for holding fresh water needed during the tea ceremony

mizuya: teahouse kitchen

natsume: type of tea container usually made out of wood and lacquered; used for light tea

nijiri guchi: small entrance to the tea room; *nijiri* means "to slide" and *guchi* means "entrance"

oolong: type of Chinese tea

roji: garden pathway to the tearoom

sei: cleanliness or purity

sencha: a type of green tea; *sen* means "boil"

shifuku: special bags for covering chaire tea containers, which are used only for thick tea

shoji: sliding doors or windows covered with shoji paper

tenmoku: a perfectly shaped tea bowl on a stand

tobi ishi: stepping-stones

tskukubai: stone basin in the garden; generally a low basin, so one must stoop down to use it

tokonoma: an alcove built in a room and raised about three to four inches above the floor to display the arts

To-o Cha: tea-drinking contest played in the fourteenth and fifteenth centuries

usucha: light tea

wa: harmony

yoritsuki: the receiving room or space where guests prepare themselves

Blue and White America Japanese Antiques
www.trocader.com/blueandwhiteamerica

Boneyard Pottery
www.boneyardpottery.com

D. Michael Coffee Ceramics
www.dmcarts.com

Japanese Green Tea Online
www.japanesegreentea.com

Matcha and More
www.matchaandmore.com

The Tea Ceramics of Richard Milgrim
www.holymtn.com/teaceramics/index_teabowl.html

Tea Circle
www.tea-circle.com

Tea Shop Horaido
www.kyoto-teramachi.or.jp/horaido/greentea.htm

Tea Toys
www.teatoys.com

tea equipment resources